CW00683638

FIELD GUIDE TO BRITISH DEER

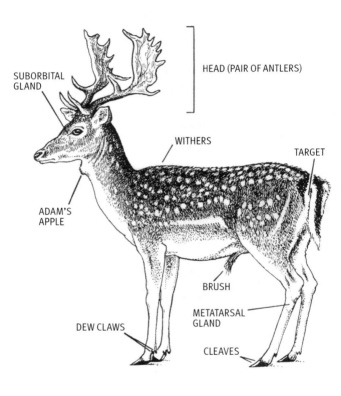

SUBORBITAL GLAND

HEAD (PAIR OF ANTLERS)

WITHERS

TARGET

ADAM'S APPLE

BRUSH

METATARSAL GLAND

DEW CLAWS

CLEAVES

Fallow buck in late summer

FIELD GUIDE TO BRITISH DEER

Fourth edition

Revised and edited by
Charles Smith-Jones

Illustrated by
Katie Hargreaves and Michael Clark

the british
deer society
DIAMOND ANNIVERSARY

Coch-y-Bonddu Books
2023

FIELD GUIDE TO BRITISH DEER

This edition © Coch-y-Bonddu Books Ltd 2023
Text © The British Deer Society 2023
First published 1967
Second edition 1971
Third edition 1982
Fourth edition 2023

ISBN: 978-1-915714-04-6

Coch-y-Bonddu Books Ltd
Machynlleth, Powys, SY20 8DG
0044 (0)1654 702837
www.anglebooks.com

CONTENTS

INTRODUCTION

The Field Guide to British Deer made its first appearance in 1957, at a time when the true status of wild deer across the United Kingdom was not fully understood. The book was put together by a small number of enthusiasts belonging to the Deer Group of the Mammal Society. The formation of the British Deer Society (BDS), which grew out of the Mammal Society in 1963, along with a growing interest among naturalists, photographers, film makers, artists and others has contributed to our combined knowledge since then. Increased and continuing academic research into the behaviour, parasitology, pathology and physiology of deer, as well as regular nationwide distribution surveys, carried out by the BDS and others, has also added to the available information on British deer species.

The original intention in 1957 was to produce a simple guide to the study of deer and as such the *Guide* certainly achieved its aims. It is a measure of its success that much of the content remains unchanged (although as our knowledge of deer has grown there have been subsequent revised and updated editions). Additionally, much has changed in the British landscape over the years and, perhaps surprisingly, deer have largely benefitted from these changes. As post-war tree planting programmes were established and came to fruition, new habitats were created and the deer flourished. Against this, an increase in built-up areas has forced deer to adapt to the presence of humans in and around their natural habitat, and deer species are now frequently encountered in urban gardens and parks. Although it is virtually impossible to accurately count wild deer populations, there is little doubt that there are more deer living across the UK today than there have been for the past 1000 years.

The first edition of the *Guide* focused on five deer species, the indigenous red and roe, the fallow (which has been with us so long, since its introduction by the Normans, that it is almost treated as an honorary native), and the sika and muntjac, new arrivals from Asia in the late nineteenth century. Then the numbers of non-native deer caused little concern; today the situation is different. Increasing sika numbers bring fears over hybridisation with native red deer, and the muntjac has recently found itself denounced as an invasive alien. The water deer, another newcomer, was found only in limited areas in the late 1950s and received scant attention, but it too has spread and established in new parts of the country. This new edition of the *Guide* takes all of the changes into account and adds new material. It should also be noted that although domesticated reindeer roam free in the Cairngorms of Scotland, as they are not truly wild deer they do not fall within the scope of this *Guide*.

An important change to deer welfare occurred soon after the initial 1957 publication with the passing by Parliament of the Deer (Scotland) Act 1959 and the Deer Act 1963. These finally gave deer, which had until then been persecuted and treated as little better than vermin in many places, much needed protection in the form of close seasons and the stipulation of basic requirements as to how they might be controlled where necessary. This foundation legislation, amended and improved to meet the needs of the modern world, remains in place today.

It is hoped that this updated *Guide* will continue to inspire new generations of deer enthusiasts and help introduce them to the pleasure of watching and studying these inspiring, elusive and iconic animals. A Glossary of terms for each section can be found on pp 82–88.

The BDS works tirelessly to promote deer conservation, education, research and management best practice to ensure a healthy and sustainable deer population, in balance with the environment, as a key feature of the UK landscape. It is perhaps fitting that this revised and up-to-date edition of the *Guide* comes on the 60th anniversary of the Society's formation.

The Introduction to the 1957 edition concluded with some essential advice for the deer watcher that is as good today as it was then, so once again it is included here:

Above all things, let not the devil tempt you to trifle with a deer's nose. You may cross his sight, walk up to him in a grey coat, or if standing against a tree or rock near your own colour, wait till he walks up to you, but you cannot cross his nose even at an incredible distance, but he will feel the tainted air. Colours and forms may be deceptive or alike; there are grey, brown and green rocks and stocks as well as man – and all these may be equivocal – but there is one scent of Man and that he never doubts or mistakes; that is filled with danger and terror; and one whiff of its poison a mile off – his nose to the wind – and the next moment his antlers turn and he is away to the hill or wood – and he cannot be seen on the same side of the forest for a month.

J Sobieski, and C Stuart, *Lays of the Deer Forest*, 1848

HOW TO USE THE FIELD GUIDE

Unless you have beginner's luck you may not necessarily find it easy to see deer at your first attempt. To improve your chances, you need to follow a few simple rules, and with practice regular success should follow.

First, you need to confirm the *Distribution* of the various deer species in your area by checking the maps on pages 75-80, taking into account the *Habitat* preferred by each as found on pages 15-18. This will give you an idea of where, and in what type of country, you are likely to find the deer that you are looking for. Then take a preliminary walk looking for the *Signs of the Presence of Deer* described on pages 12-15.

The clearest indications of the presence of deer are the *Tracks* that they make. These are described and illustrated on pages 18-25. Be careful not to confuse the tracks of deer with those left by cattle, sheep or other livestock. With experience you should find that you can follow deer paths successfully through woodland. This will tell you much about how deer live and the places most used in their activities at the time of year when you visit.

Look also for *Droppings* like those shown on pages 27-30. These will give you a little help in confirming the species, size and sometimes the sex of the deer present, but approach the evidence with caution and do not rely solely upon it.

The real excitement and interest will come when you see your first wild deer. You must follow the rules concerning approach and observation (pages 32-34). Deer have highly developed senses of smell, hearing and sight. As you may get only glimpses of your quarry, the sounds made by deer can be very important. *Voice* (pages 36-39) describes the various calls that they make throughout the year, and especially those made if they see you before you see them. The *Identification* features on pages 40-43 and photographs between pages 80 and 81 will greatly assist in confirming your observations, and take special note of the appearance of deer as it can change with the seasons.

Once you have learned how to find and approach your deer you will want to know more about them. *Antler Development and Age* (pages 44-49), *Seasonal Changes of Coat* (pages 53-55) and *Gait* (pages 56-58) all provide additional means of identification and will extend your interest.

If you intend to make a special study of deer, you will need to know about their *Feeding Habits* (pages 59-61) and their *Herd Activities* (pages 62-67). Annual variations in habits and activities are shown in the *Seasonal Behaviour* charts (pages 69-73).

You may find it very helpful to keep notes and sketches of what you see, setting them down at once if possible. A small camera, or one on a mobile phone, is very useful in this respect. Towards the back of this Guide you will find a Glossary of technical and other terms used to describe deer and their surroundings, which will help in ensuring that your descriptions are clear and concise, along with suggested sources of information should you decide to extend your studies.

SIGNS OF THE PRESENCE OF DEER

Once a possible location for deer has been identified, preliminary investigations can be very helpful in confirming their presence and even what species are likely to be found there. Look for the following:

Tracks: The most significant and useful evidence. See p 18.

Droppings: Important but caution needed. See p 27.

Creeps and runways: Deer make regular use of paths, often parallel to those used by human beings but 10 m or so into cover, leading to significant areas such as feeding grounds, rutting stands or resting places. Look for entry points into thick undergrowth, creeps under fences or work trackways down banks. Narrow pathways in thick, low vegetation may suggest the presence of muntjac.

Fraying stocks: Freshly marked trees are a very good indication of the recent presence of deer and may suggest a territorial animal. Those found from April to July are almost certainly made by roe deer, while muntjac may fray all year round. A roe fraying stock often has a scrape at the base, sometimes with the imprint of a stamped forefoot. See p 65.

Fraying height, main periods and causes														
	Height (m)	Jan	Feb	Mar	Apr	May	Jun	Jul	Aug	Sep	Oct	Nov	Dec
Red	1.8							Velvet removal			Territorial		
Sika	1.6							Velvet removal		Territorial			
Fallow	1.6						Velvet removal			Territorial			
Roe	0.8		Velvet removal				Territorial						
Muntjac	0.2 to 0.5							Velvet removal					
		Territorial											
Water deer	0.5											Territorial	

Thrashed bushes and rubbed trees: See pp 63-64.

Bark stripping: A particular habit of red and fallow deer, and occasionally sika, in late winter and early spring.

Bole scoring of larger trees: The scoring of bark with antlers, most characteristically done by sika, although occasionally also by red and fallow deer.

Ground scrapes and pits: Deer may scrape the ground vigorously with a forefoot, often as part of territorial marking. On a larger scale are the stamping grounds of small herds of sika, fallow and red deer, and assemblies on a relatively small patch of ground can produce considerable disturbance. This may sometimes be around a prominent object such as a tree stump, bole of a tree or even a telegraph pole.

Bedding places: Areas corresponding roughly with the size of the animal, and sometimes associated with flattening or discolouration of the grass. Fallow deer may use hollows full of dead leaves. Both sexes of roe have been known to build up "back rests" from loose debris on the windward side of bedding places.

Wallows: These are peat, water and/or mud-filled hollows used by sika and red deer during the rut. They usually show signs of considerable regular activity. Wallows may also be used by both sexes during spring and summer.

Cast hair: Look for signs of hair from deer on barbed wire fences, particularly where deer pass under wire. Cast hair can also be found in bedding places, and wallows often contain large amounts.

Play and rutting rings: Fallow and roe deer make these. Play rings are used by fallow bucks in February and March, and by does and kids in August and September. Roe rings are made and used by does and kids during June and early July. During the rut the roe buck may chase the doe and produce well-worn circular or figure-of-eight pathways around a focal point such as a tree or bush. Early rutting rings made in early July tend to be larger than those made as the rut peaks in late July and early August.

Browsing: Careful examination of plants will show where stems have been cut within a deer's reach. Where deer numbers are high this may result in a very obvious browse line on vegetation. Care should be taken not to confuse deer browsing with that of rabbits and hares: the former make a clean cut while deer, which have no upper  incisors, create a more ragged cut and tear.

HABITAT

The natural habitat of most deer is wooded country with thick cover. If they are unmolested they may be seen grazing or resting in more open conditions, and where mountain and moorland exist red, sika and even roe deer may seek the cooler conditions they offer to avoid the attention of insects. Deer may move considerable distances, often at night. Some, particularly the roe and muntjac, are increasingly encountered in gardens and semi-urban areas where they are content to live as long as they have appropriate food and cover and are left relatively undisturbed.

This section will be found useful in relation to those on *Habits* and *Herd Activities* on pages 62-67 and the *Seasonal Behaviour Charts* on pages 69 to 73.

RED DEER

Native to the margins of large forests. In Britain they inhabit woodlands with thick cover, and moorlands or uncultivated country near to woodlands. Where natural forest has been removed, as in much of Scotland and parts of England and Ireland, they have become secondarily adapted to the exposed conditions  of mountain and glen. In hot weather, when it is possible, they lie up in heather on open hillsides and mountain tops where the air is cool and attack by insects is less severe.

Winter ranges are usually on lower sheltered ground.

SIKA

Appear to prefer areas with acid heathland soil. Lie up mainly in woodland during daylight hours, especially wherever thick cover is provided by dense hazel thickets, bramble brakes, tall bracken, rhododendron clumps and unbrashed conifer plantations. May also be found in marshy localities such as alder carrs and estuarine reed beds.

In warm weather, when troubled by biting insects, sika may harbour in tall corn or other field crops, and where little persecution exists they may wander abroad by day on moor and heathland. Where mountain deer forest exists, they may seek the high tops rather like red deer.

FALLOW DEER

Most frequently found in lowland woods, predominantly of older hardwood trees providing thick cover. Where deer parks have existed or still exist, feral herds are likely in surrounding areas.

May be seen feeding along woodland margins or rides, and in fields nearby, at dawn and dusk. In undisturbed localities they may even feed or lie out in the open during the day.

The oldest bucks tend to be almost entirely nocturnal and are only infrequently seen outside the rut.

ROE DEER

Usually found in young plantations before the thicket stage and in woodlands with plenty of undergrowth and close to more open grassy areas, forest clearings or cultivated ground. In summer, seeks cool, leafy shade in bracken or other dense vegetation. May sometimes be flushed from bedding places, and if startled will seek safety in flight during which a series of sharp barks may be given (see p 38).

Where population densities are high, roe may be found in all types of woodland both large and small, and anywhere else where cover and seclusion are adequate, such as isolated thickets and shelter belts, moorland scrub or coastal undercliffs. It is not unusual for roe to be found lying out in open Scottish deer forest more usually inhabited by red deer.

Early morning and dusk provide chances to observe these deer feeding in forest rides or in open places. After rain is a particularly good time. Where seldom disturbed, roe can be seen fairly frequently by day, sometimes with cattle. In winter they lie up in denser woodland, especially where there are Douglas firs or unbrashed pine trees.

Where reed beds exist alongside a forested area some roe are likely to be found. A marsh or other source of water will attract these deer, although there are some places such as woodlands on chalk downland, and scrub on limestone pavement, where many roe live remote from surface water and where the only sources of supply are dew and in the food taken.

MUNTJAC

Primarily found in woods with low, tangled brambles and similar undergrowth, this species is seldom found far from cover. Muntjac are easily hidden and may exist undetected under such conditions for a considerable time. Their presence may be betrayed if narrow runways are found. It is less likely if there is a close canopy and little ground cover. They may live temporarily in standing crops.

Most frequently seen in the evening and very early morning in open grassy places or nearby cultivated fields where feeding is likely to occur but they regularly feed in dense cover as well. Acorns, chestnuts and crab apples are attractive to these small deer and they should be looked for where such supplies exist in autumn.

Muntjac can sometimes be flushed from dense brambles during winter time. Regularly used pathways may then more easily be found leading to feeding places and bedding areas. Look for their *Tracks* (p 24) and *Droppings* (p 29).

WATER DEER

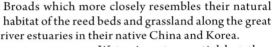

Prefer the habitat offered by fenland reed beds and the Norfolk Broads which more closely resembles their natural habitat of the reed beds and grassland along the great river estuaries in their native China and Korea.

Water is not essential but they do like thick cover in which to lie up. They have adapted well to parkland with its associated woods, and can also be found, sometimes in high numbers, in arable fields divided by thick hedges that provide cover.

TRACKS

The first indication of the presence of deer in an unfamiliar area will probably be provided by their tracks. The ability to read them accurately is essential for those who wish to study these elusive animals, and with some initial instruction and practice it is possible to become proficient. A tape measure, or folding rule, allows the tracks of any deer seen to be carefully measured and recorded (a pair of dividers are also very useful for accuracy).

The recognition of fresh tracks will provide information as to the places most frequented by deer and where they may best be watched for. Detailed examination will reveal variations in the size, shape and arrangement of the tracks, leading eventually to an understanding of the gait and positive identification of the species. The final achievement is being able to estimate from tracks the sex and approximate number of deer in a particular area.

This is done through a process known as "ringing" or making a circuit of the area, and is best carried out at dawn or as soon as the deer have settled for the day. New tracks show up well in dew or hoar-frost, or after a fine night following rain or snow. The freshness of a track is gauged by making a mark beside it, and then comparing its appearance with that of the track. Slots show up more plainly when viewed against the low sun of morning. After a dew, grass holds down when trodden. If deer are being followed when this has occurred the tracks look light, but if the observer is moving in the opposite direction to the deer the tracks show up darker.

All passes, entries, galleries and racks (see *Glossary* p 82) are checked and foiled tracks (tracks in grass) followed up until slots are found. Individual tracks are memorised and the number entering an area balanced against those leaving it. Large areas are ringed in sections by following rides and streams, but always working upwind so that deer are not moved onto ground which has yet to be searched.

Where several deer species are present it may be more appropriate to undertake an impact assessment which takes tracks, dung, bite marks, fraying and other signs of deer presence into account. Conducted regularly, such assessments allow changes in deer numbers and impacts to be evaluated across a given area over a period of time.

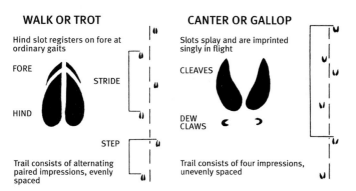

WALK OR TROT

Hind slot registers on fore at ordinary gaits

FORE

STRIDE

HIND

STEP

Trail consists of alternating paired impressions, evenly spaced

CANTER OR GALLOP

Slots splay and are imprinted singly in flight

CLEAVES

DEW CLAWS

Trail consists of four impressions, unevenly spaced

The tracks of deer differ from those of cloven-hoofed domestic animals (cattle, sheep, goats and pigs) as follows:

- The slots are narrow in proportion, the cleaves taper to a point and the heels are rounded, never sharply defined.
- The tread is mainly on the toes, and the cleaves normally close along their whole length, splaying only in soft ground or when in flight.
- The hind feet register consistently and more or less completely at ordinary gaits.
- The prints lie more or less closely along one median line.
- The step is relatively long in proportion to the size of the foot.

The form of the slot and the pattern of the trail are modified not only by gait but also by size, age, type of ground, condition and sex. In doubtful instances the effect of these must be understood and taken into account before a definitive identification of the species can be made. Among the larger species of deer, individual variation is usually sufficiently marked to enable the tracks of one animal to be followed among others of the same kind and to be recognised again later on. Final judgement must never be given on a few slots, but only after the trail has been followed sufficiently to show which features are consistent and reliable.

Slot and gait: In all species except muntjac there is no general difference (except perhaps an individual one) between the slot of opposite sides. There is often some difference in shape between the fore and hind slot, however, and in all species the hind slot is rather shorter than the fore. As the hind slots come uppermost when the prints register, they serve as the main basis of comparison. Their shape, size, depth and position are all significant. Variations in gait do not assist much with identification, and the principal comparisons must always be related to the normal walking pace. This is recognised by a regular step and consistent registration, with all the prints falling neatly into line. In these conditions, the length of step is constant for each individual; this and the width of the slot across the heel are the key measurements.

Terrain: The influence of ground conditions on the form and pattern of the tracks becomes evident to a practiced observer.

The effects are discounted by following each trail as far as possible across different types of ground until a fair sample of tracks have been examined, and their normal appearance can be deduced. The softer the ground, the larger the print.

Size and age: In a young deer, the slots are small, shallow and short; tread is on the toes, and the cleaves are sharp pointed and normally shut. In an old deer the slots are large, deep and long; tread is more on the heels and the cleaves are worn and blunt. They tend to splay, and the fore cleaves are often kept open.

The step of a young deer is short and that of an old deer is long. This difference increases with the pace and when moving together, the younger is usually the first to change gait. At a normal walk, the average stride is roughly equal to the height of the shoulder; a young deer tends to over-reach slightly but consistently with the hind feet while an old deer consistently steps short.

Condition: This varies according to season. In a fat beast, or a female at an advanced stage of pregnancy, the hind slots are placed somewhat to the side of the fore, the prints are deeper, and the sway is increased. The fatter the deer the greater the sway. With animals in poor condition, such as males exhausted after the rut, the hind slots drop behind those of the fore, and may even fail to register altogether.

Sex: Difference in the tracks are slight between the sexes when young but become more definite with age. In two animals of differing age showing the same length of step, the younger animal is the male, eg the step of a four-year red stag is about the same as that of an old hind. As a rule the slots and step of a mature male are some one-fifth greater than those of a mature female of the same species. His far heavier weight helps to develop other characteristics.

Thus his slots are longer and deeper, and in proportion relatively broader. His fore slots are relatively longer in proportion to his hind, and the fore cleaves show a tendency to splay. The shape of the cleaves is more obtuse, and their edges are less sharp. In species which use them, the dew claws are larger in proportion, more prominent and less sharp; they splay more widely, pointing outwards rather than downwards.

His step is not only longer but more regular, the sway is

normally greater, and he tends to point his toes outwards. In the female, registration is frequently more accurate but generally less consistent, her step is uneven and the toes normally point directly forward.

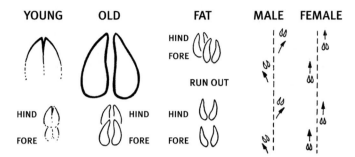

YOUNG   OLD   FAT   MALE   FEMALE

Identification of tracks

The diagrams that follow show the tracks of the hind foot of a mature male deer of each species, for comparison of size and shape. The average length of step is given in the accompanying descriptions below. These also refer to mature males in each instance. All dimensions are approximate.

The tracks of females and young have the characteristic shape somewhat modified by the factors given on pages 20 and 21 but they are still recognisable if these factors are correctly taken into account. Allowance must be made for a proportionate reduction in the size of slot and the length of step.

Red

7 cm

Roe

Fallow

Sika

Muntjac

Left   Right

Water deer

Male hind foot track at approximately 80% full size

Dimensions of individual slots and stride

	Slot length	Width at heel	Step length (walking)	Comments
Red	8 cm	6 cm	60 cm or more	Fore and hind slot not dissimilar. Cleaves short in proportion, somewhat rounded, and can splay even when walking. Marks of dew claws prominent when running.
Sika	8 cm	5 cm	45 cm	Fore cleaves elongated and tend to splay. Hind cleaves short and rounded, normally shut at heel. Marks of dew claws frequent.
Fallow	6.5 cm	5 cm	52 cm	Fore and hind slots not dissimilar. Cleaves long in proportion, somewhat straight-sided and have little tendency to splay. Marks of dew claws rare.
Roe	4–5 cm	3.5 cm	37 cm	Fore and hind slots not dissimilar. Cleaves narrow in proportion, evenly tapered, somewhat open at the heel with much tendency to splay. Dew claws often show on soft ground and can be prominent when the animal is running. Slots of kids may be confused with those of muntjac in early summer.
Muntjac	3 cm	2 cm	30 cm	Very small slots. Cleaves may register unevenly with median cleave slighter, but often symmetrical. Dew claws register only occasionally in soft mud.
Water deer	5 cm	3 cm	35 cm	Slot long, pointed and narrow. Deep impression of a splayed foot often shows a web-like structure between the toes. Dew claws register in snow or soft mud.
Sheep	6 cm	4.5 cm	40 cm	Very dependent on breed; toes tend to splay outwards when walking and very obviously when running.
Goat	6 cm	5 cm	60 cm	Dependent on breed. Inside edges of cleaves notably concave.

Comparison with domestic animals

In all cases aspects can vary according to breed as well as age and sex. The following diagrams are given only as examples and may not be typical in every locality. The prints of some breeds can be more deer-like in appearance, others less so. The examples below are of adult males (hind foot) in each instance as these tend to be more common and the most deer-like.

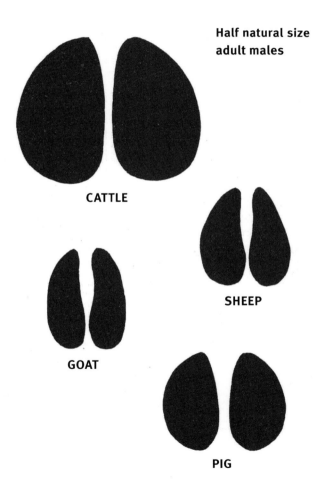

**Half natural size
adult males**

CATTLE

SHEEP

GOAT

PIG

How to Make a Plaster Cast of the Track of a Deer

Carefully remove twigs, leaves or mud that have fallen into the print. Forceps or photographers' blower brush are useful at this stage.

Mix plaster of Paris with clean water in plastic bowl.

Press card (or tin) strip round track and avoid air bubbles by pouring plaster carefully onto side of track.

Check by gentle finger pressure to see if dry. This usually takes 15-30 minutes depending on how much water was mixed with plaster.

Cut out soil round plaster and remove complete. Pull back card and pack carefully inside newspaper.

Very gently wash off mud under tap. When dry, colour track or back-ground and add details.

DROPPINGS

The droppings of deer are another good indicator of their presence. Individually they are more properly known as *fewmets*, or in groups as *crotties*. Fresh ones can range in colour between green, brown and black, but are usually glossy and smooth-looking with one end pointed and the other slightly concave. After a day or two they start to dry out and become duller and may even change colour. Care must be taken not to confuse them with the droppings of goats or sheep, but the droppings of rabbits and hares, in contrast, are round, fibrous and unmistakeable.

Unlike the leavings of many other animals, the dung of deer is quite innocuous and having plant material as its source smells very little, usually of grass. If you need to handle droppings, though, do take care to wear disposable gloves. Like other animals, deer carry the bacterium *E.coli* 0157 in their gut. This can pose a serious health risk to humans, although it is easily avoided by taking suitable precautions and maintaining good personal hygiene.

The size of deer droppings will vary according to the age, sex and condition of an individual animal even within species. Normally dropped as firm pellets, those of an animal in high condition (such as a red stag before the rut) can be loose and resemble small cow pats. An animal which has been feeding heavily on a flush of new growth after the harder months of winter can also produce very loose droppings when the bacteria in the gut essential to digestion have not had a chance to accustom to a radical change of diet; at such times some deer, and especially roe, can experience quite severe diarrhoea.

Sometimes droppings are found in adherent clusters rather than as individual pellets, or left in a string along trails by moving animals. Some species appear to use regular latrine areas, often close to their bedding places, where large accumulations of their droppings can build up. Always allow for size, particularly from May to December when immature animals are growing up.

The following drawings are rendered approximately at their average natural size.

Red deer   2–3 cm, light brown to black when fresh

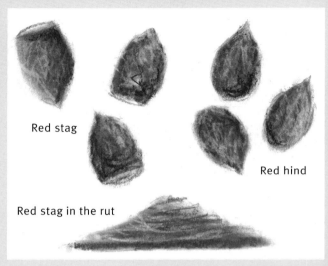

Red stag

Red hind

Red stag in the rut

Colour can vary greatly. The pointed opposite end generally fits into the concavity of the previous dropping but these indentations are not always clear. Around June the heaps of fewmets (crotties) can be frequently adherent; in July individual fewmets are longer and harder. Pre-rut stag droppings can resemble miniature cow pats around 5–8 cm across. During the rut they become small and misshapen as the stag is taking very little food.

Fallow deer   1–1.5 cm, black when fresh

Buck

Doe

Look glossy when fresh. Sometimes adherent and faceted. Droppings of bucks are usually concave at one end. Those of does are more flattened. Often in heaps but may be left in a string if the animal is moving.

Sika 1–1.5 cm
Shiny green or brown when fresh

Frequently found in heaps and often deposited in latrine piles close to bedding areas. Usually not adherent. Become black when old. Can be difficult to distinguish from roe, though stag droppings larger.

Roe deer 1–1.5 cm
Dark brown or black when fresh

Only very rarely adherent. Usually single but often accumulated near bedding places. Somewhat glossy and similar in appearance for both sexes; slightly thinner than sika.

Muntjac 1 cm
Shiny black when fresh

Faceted with small terminal point. Usually spread as individual pellets, often in considerable numbers over a small area. Latrines occur at high deer densities, often next to trees. Same appearance in both sexes.

Water deer 1.5 cm
Dark brown or black when fresh

More elongated than those of other deer. Generally not adherent, but may occasionally adhere in clumps. May sometimes be shorter and difficult to distinguish from muntjac.

Other species for comparison

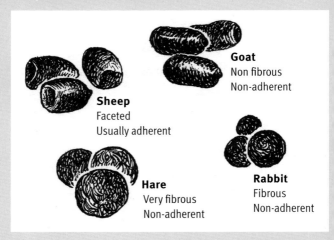

Goat
Non fibrous
Non-adherent

Sheep
Faceted
Usually adherent

Rabbit
Fibrous
Non-adherent

Hare
Very fibrous
Non-adherent

It can be very easy to misidentify the droppings of deer, but with experience they can become a useful guide to the species in a given area and give you a good idea of how recently they visited it. It is essential though to remain aware, however, that they are only a guide. There can be much similarity between the droppings of the young of a larger species and those of an adult smaller one (eg fallow and roe respectively). Some woodland managers and scientists have developed methods of analysing accumulations of deer dung in set locations to determine numbers for census purposes.

AN INTRODUCTION TO DEER WATCHING

The hints on watching deer in this section are intended to provide useful guidance to the newcomer.

Clothing

Clothing should be comfortable and adapted to the season and weather. Colours need to blend with the surroundings and materials should allow easy, silent movement. Any noisy clothing is not suitable. As deer, unlike humans, are able to detect ultra-violet light, clothes washed in many modern washing powders with brightening agents will be more visible to them.

Drab coloured garments in olive green, khaki or green and brown mixtures are generally suitable, the important thing being to try to merge into the background. A hat of some kind provides shade for eyes and also shadows and camouflages the face, while gloves help to conceal the tell-tale movement of hands as binoculars are raised and lowered. Footwear should be as light as practical to allow the wearer to move silently, although for rough or mountainous ground heavier boots with good grip and ankle support are recommended.

Equipment

Good quality binoculars are essential. Clear vision in poor light is more important than high magnification. 7x or 8x are suitable magnifications, coupled with an object lens that optimises light transmission; overall weight should be not be burdensome to carry. A small camera, such as that found on a mobile telephone, is useful for recording findings, as are a notebook and pencil. The serious deer photographer will require a telephoto facility with a wide aperture, and a small portable tripod or a support pole is almost essential.

A day sack or a "bum bag" is useful for small items of equipment but many find that they can carry all they need in the pockets of a suitable jacket. Insect repellent can be important, and a tape measure or suitably marked stick will find frequent use for taking measurements. Avoid anything that rustles, rattles or shines.

Remote wildlife cameras, which are triggered by a passing deer or other animal, are useful for recording wildlife movements during both day and night, but care should be taken to site them away from casual view if they are not to be tampered with or even stolen. Modern portable thermal imaging devices are increasingly available and help detect the heat signatures of animals, not visible to the naked eye, in conditions ranging from daylight to full darkness.

Tactics

Successful deer watching tactics will vary according to the type of country. A careful, quiet approach is always necessary, using whatever cover is available and taking the wind direction into careful consideration as a deer's nose will detect human scent at very long distances. It is often better to remain static in a fixed observation point and wait for the deer to show themselves, usually at dawn or dusk. Building a temporary hide can be helpful and lightweight portable ones are available. Otherwise the observer may prefer to stalk likely areas, moving extremely slowly and stopping to observe frequently. A deer watcher needs to be able to remain motionless when necessary, as even the slightest movement can cause an alert deer to move off.

Deer can often be surprisingly difficult to detect against their surroundings. Look for shapes and colours that seem out of place, such as the horizontal line of a back or a white rump patch, and be alert to slight movements like the twitch of an ear. Your aim is always to outwit the superb senses of smell and hearing that deer possess. Although their eyesight can be poor at all but the closest ranges, they are very quick to spot movement even at longer distances.

Always stalk as closely into the wind as possible and check its direction frequently with a wetted finger or by dropping dried grass. Spend time looking and listening and try to remain in shadow, remaining well balanced while moving so that you can stand still instantly in case you need to freeze. Avoid open spaces, and if you cannot avoid crossing one spend some time spying from cover first. Deer may often spend time in the open drying themselves after a period of rain.

Many noises are alien to the woods, such as coughing, loud talking or metallic sounds, but the knock of a stick against another wooden object is more natural. If this happens simply stand quietly for a while before continuing and try not to repeat it. Deer can make a considerable amount of noise themselves if they are confident in their surroundings and, if careful, you may hear them before you see them. A moving bush or sapling branches may betray the presence of a fraying or feeding animal.

Above all, the better you get to know the ground the more successful you are likely to be. The best times for a foot stalk are in the early morning just before dawn and for an hour or so after it, or the period leading up to and beyond dusk. There are places where deer can be seen throughout the day, especially where they are undisturbed or during the rut. Do take care not to follow them into their sanctuaries or onto rutting stands, however. A deer aware of human presence is likely to seek dense cover, and repeated disturbance may cause them to leave an area altogether.

If you sight a deer, stand still unless you are in good cover yourself, and do not move until it has its head down feeding or is facing directly away from you. A deer's eyes are situated on the side of its head and give excellent all-round vision. It should not be necessary to approach any deer to closer than around 50 m, and if you can depart without making the deer aware of your presence so much the better. The less they know that they have been observed, the more likely it will be that future opportunities will be possible. If the deer are on the move, the wind is in your favour, and you stand perfectly still, it is quite possible for them to pass very close without detecting you.

High seats

A high seat is often by far the best way to watch deer. The observer, sited well above ground level, is static and far less visible (although deer may still pick up any fidgeting movements), human scent tends to be carried away above ground level, and fields of view may be greatly improved.

There are various types of high seat which can be bought ready-made or constructed from locally available materials such as cut and treated wood. Some are designed to use a suitable tree for support, while others may be free-standing. Designs which enclose the observer in a roofed box offer shelter from the weather and give shade that helps to camouflage the occupant. If there is appropriate raised ground a low seat or "doe box" – an enclosed structure at ground level – may provide a suitable alternative. All should be regularly checked to ensure that they are serviceable and carry a warning sign prohibiting unauthorised use; it is always best to site high seats out of sight of places regularly used by the public, such as footpaths and other rights of way.

Siting a high seat to best effect demands a thorough knowledge of the area involved and the habits of local deer including tracks, feeding places, assembly areas and rutting grounds. Never site a high seat too close to a deer path; it needs to be several metres to one side of it. Take careful note of prevailing winds and ensure that there is a clear route into it to permit an undetected approach.

When using any type of seat or ground hide, it is essential to be in position long before you expect the deer to be moving so that the surrounding area can settle down after being temporarily disturbed by your movements getting to it.

THREE STEEL MANUFACTURED HIGH SEATS

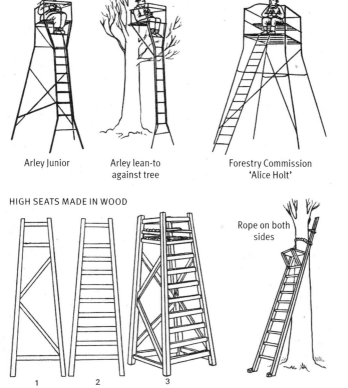

Arley Junior

Arley lean-to
against tree

Forestry Commission
'Alice Holt'

HIGH SEATS MADE IN WOOD

Rope on both
sides

1   2   3

1 & 2 are made first. 3 shows the completed
seat (after the Forestry Commission leaflet
No 52: *The Fallow Deer* by WA Cadman BA)

Ladder seat supported
by two struts with rope
round tree

VOICE

Deer are generally quiet animals. Alarmed deer generally choose to depart unobtrusively but may issue a vocal warning to others of a potentially dangerous intruder in their vicinity. An observer who has been detected by an unseen deer may at least be able to identify it by the sound it makes.

The males of most deer species make characteristic calls during the rut. Females and young will maintain contact with each other using various bleating or piping calls.

RED DEER

This species is characteristically silent apart from during the rut.

During the rut the stag roars, especially around first and last light. The sound resembles the bellow of a bull but with a deeper intonation, and usually ends with several grunts. Woodland stags often give a single resonant groan at long intervals. During the rest of the year the stag may make a rare warning bark if alarmed, and grunts when troubled by flies.

The hind likewise makes little sound except for a gruff bark to her calf when returning to it. She may also make a more frequent nasal call, and utters a crisp warning bark if suddenly disturbed or unsure of a potential threat that she cannot identify.

The calf has a high-pitched bleat and screams if alarmed.

SIKA

For most of the year this species is generally silent unless alarmed.

The rutting call of the stag is impossible to confuse with any of the UK's other deer. It consists of a carrying whistle, rising to a crescendo and descending again to a concluding grunt, usually issued three or four times in rapid succession. The stag then remains silent for the next ten to fifteen minutes and often for up to half an hour. A rutting sika can be difficult to locate by its call because of these long silent intervals. (The more frequent calls of a rutting red stag or fallow buck make them easier to pinpoint.) This sound is heard chiefly at dusk or in the early morning and has been compared to the sound of a gate swinging on its hinges.

Another type of rutting call, usually made by a stag accompanied by hinds, is a single drawn out querulous whistle rising to a peak, tailing off and ending in a grunt, and is uttered every two or three minutes. A stag challenges another with a sound rather like the "raspberry" made by expelling air through closed lips. A low bleat or grunt is uttered in the vicinity of a hind in season.

Both the stag and hind when alarmed make a short, piercing whistle, sometimes ending in a grunt, often repeated several times with a space of some fifteen to twenty seconds between calls. The hind makes a similar sound when guiding its calf though undergrowth. It is used most frequently in summer and can carry distances of up to half a mile. Stags have been heard to make a peevish squeal, especially during high winds.

When in heat, sika hinds have a special plaintive and subdued bleat which appears to be irresistible to an unmated stag.

The calf bleats in a similar manner to a fallow fawn; the sound can be imitated by blowing on a blade of grass held between the thumbs.

FALLOW DEER

This is another species that is generally quiet when adult.

The typical voice of a fallow buck during the rut is a rather fast and continuous groaning or belching with a marked rhythmic intonation. In still weather it can be heard half a mile away. A doe, and particularly one with a fawn, gives a crisp and resonant bark as a warning call if disturbed; a buck may utter a similar bark especially during rutting time. The doe makes a whining bleat when communicating with or searching for her fawn.

Fawns communicate with does using a plaintive nasal bleating "mee-ulk" which increases if they are pestered by bucks.

ROE DEER

A buck challenging an intruder utters a loud, staccato "bo…bo…bo" bark similar to that of a collie dog. Both buck and doe can make a more drawn out "bao…bao…bao" warning bark, often uttered as the animal takes flight and which coincides with the animals' bounding pace. The bark of the buck is gruff, shorter and less continuous than that of the doe which is higher pitched. Barking often continues as the animal moves off into the distance. As a general rule, the deeper the call, the older the deer. During the rut the buck grunts when pursuing a doe or a rival. The doe calls to her kids with a high-pitched "pee-you" or "peep-peep". When in oestrus she makes a faint and high-pitched piping note which the buck can hear at a considerable distance and to which he usually responds immediately by coming in search of the doe. A doe hard pressed by a rutting buck and unready to mate utters a loud, two-tone distress squeak: "pee-ah".

Kids make a shrill, lamb-like bleat.

MUNTJAC

Both sexes make a single, loud and fox-like bark, less gruff than that of a roe and repeated at intervals of four to five seconds over long periods, sometimes for up to an hour. They do this when separated, disturbed, excited, advertising their presence to others of their species, or when the doe is in oestrus.

Muntjac also grunt and make clicking sounds. They also make a piercing and distressing cry if in extreme difficulty.

Does and fawns will squeak if disturbed. A fawn separated from its mother has a characteristic and pathetic bleat, uttered in a very much higher pitch, and squeals and bleats to attract its mother if in danger.

WATER DEER

Largely quiet.

Both sexes utter a harsh bark similar to that of the muntjac, but with a more rasping edge. Barking is often carried out when alarmed and may also serve other purposes. It seems to be more prevalent during the summer which suggests that it might also have something to do with maternal behaviour. Rutting bucks make a variety of clicking or chittering clicks and squeals, and courting animals may squeak.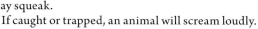

If caught or trapped, an animal will scream loudly.

Light

Thick neck

Dark underside

Mane September to November

Yellowish target

RED STAG **AUGUST TO FEBRUARY**

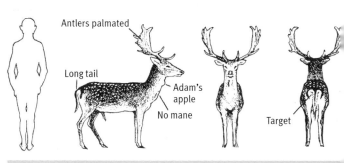

Antlers palmated

Long tail

Adam's apple

No mane

Target

FALLOW BUCK **MID-AUGUST TO APRIL**

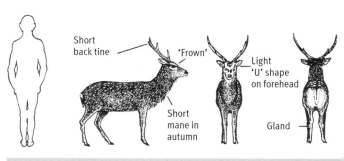

Short back tine

'Frown'

Light 'U' shape on forehead

Short mane in autumn

Gland

SIKA STAG **SEPTEMBER TO MARCH**

See also colour plates

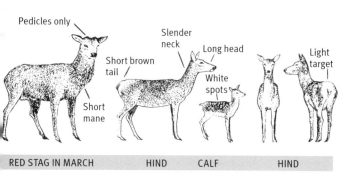

Pedicles only

Slender neck

Long head

Short brown tail

White spots

Light target

Short mane

RED STAG IN MARCH **HIND** **CALF** **HIND**

In both sexes many colour varieties including all white and all black occur.

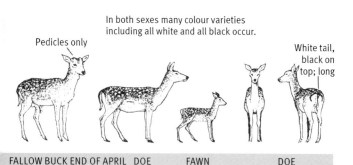

Pedicles only

White tail, black on top; long

FALLOW BUCK END OF APRIL **DOE** **FAWN** **DOE**

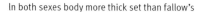

In both sexes body more thick set than fallow's

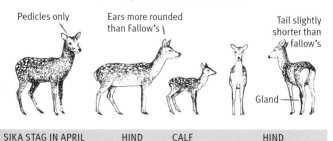

Pedicles only

Ears more rounded than Fallow's

Tail slightly shorter than fallow's

Gland

SIKA STAG IN APRIL **HIND** **CALF** **HIND**

Identification (continued)

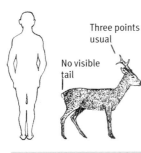 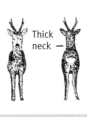 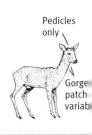

Three points usual

No visible tail

Thick neck

Pedicles only

Gorge patch variab

ROE BUCK JUNE TO OCTOBER NOVEMBER

Sexes similar size

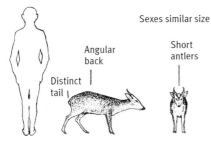  

Angular back

Distinct tail

Short antlers

Head low to body

MUNTJAC BUCK DOE

Both sexes look alike

Buck does not carry antlers

Long canine

Ears rounder than muntjac's

Shorter canine in doe

WATER DEER BUCK DOE

Sexes similar size

Spotted

Slender neck

Distinct white tuft

ROE DOE IN JUNE   **KID**   **DOE IN DECEMBER**

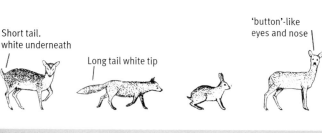

Short tail. white underneath

Long tail white tip

'button'-like eyes and nose

MUNTJAC DOE   **FOX**   **HARE**   **WATER DEER**

Herd near Aviemore, Inverness

White mane during rut

Bulls and cows bear antlers, but cow's smaller. Bulls shed December, cows after calving in spring

Short mane

REINDEER BULL   **COW**

43

ANTLER DEVELOPMENT AND AGEING

A focal point of a deer's annual lifecycle is the rut, and the production of antlers plays an important role in this. The water deer (right) is notable as being the only true deer never to grow antlers, instead possessing well developed canine tusks that are used in competition with other bucks or for self-defence. Muntjac too (left) have obvious though less pronounced canine tusks, but also possess simple antlers.

Antlers develop very rapidly; in the case of the red deer it takes only around four months. The degree of strain this places on an animal's strength is heavily influenced by the climate and food available.

Antlers are bony outgrowths from the skull which, unlike the horns of cattle, sheep, antelopes and others, are shed and regrown regularly. Antler growth and casting is controlled by a number of hormones, the principal one being the male hormone testosterone. The production of this is governed by the length of daylight hours.

Blood vessels on the surface and within the growing antler help to supply it with food and calcium salts necessary for growth. A soft furry skin called velvet covers the growing antler. When full growth is attained the blood vessels shrink in size, the velvet shrivels and dies and is frayed off by the deer. At this point the antlers are fixed to the skull by what are in effect immovable ball and socket joints.

The growth of new antlers starts almost immediately after the old antlers loosen in their sockets and eventually fall off. In most species this occurs well after the rutting season.

It is important to take special care when considering the growth of antlers, and it must be stressed that antler size and the number of tines or points are not only a poor indication of age but can also be extremely misleading.

Although as a general rule, antlers are shed and re-grown annually, exceptions do occur and their development depends on many factors, which might include health, nutrition, weather and genetics. The diagrams that follow (pp 47-48) show typical heads of the antlered deer species but there can be extensive variations and it is very rare indeed for two heads to be identical.

By the time a red deer stag reaches his fifth year he should have "all his rights" with brow, bay and tray tines on each antler. Many, however, miss a bay. The characteristics of antler form can be inherited and a male deer might transfer the ability to produce a good or bad "head" to his offspring.

How Antlers Grow

RED STAG CALF BORN MAY/JUNE   AFTER HERBERT FOOKS

January 7/8 months

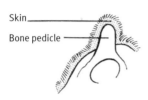

Skin

Bone pedicle

May/June
12/13 months

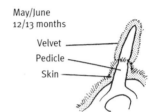

Velvet

Pedicle

Skin

July/ August 14/15 months

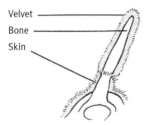

Velvet

Bone

Skin

End September
16 months

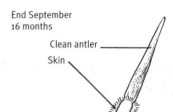

Clean antler

Skin

Stag will carry his first head
until the following March/ April

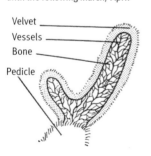

Velvet

Vessels

Bone

Pedicle

A growing antler is really the
continuation of the pedicles and
is fed by veins which lie under a
soft covering skin – velvet.

When the antler is fully formed
these recede and skin dies and
is rubbed off leaving uncovered
bone – antler.

46

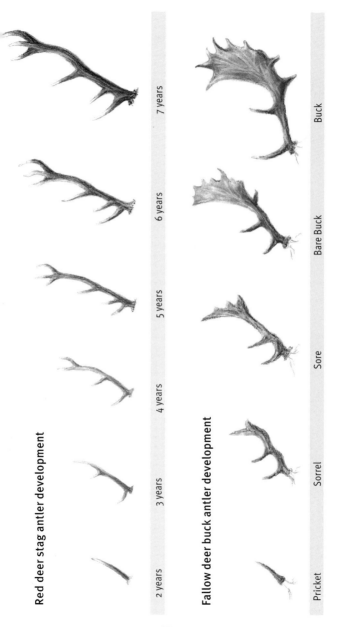

Red deer stag antler development

2 years | 3 years | 4 years | 5 years | 6 years | 7 years

Fallow deer buck antler development

Pricket | Sorrel | Sore | Bare Buck | Buck

Roe Deer Buck Antler Development

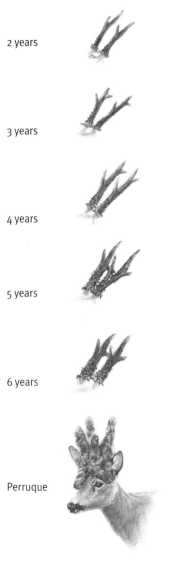

2 years

3 years

4 years

5 years

6 years

Perruque

Antler Development and Age: Muntjac Buck

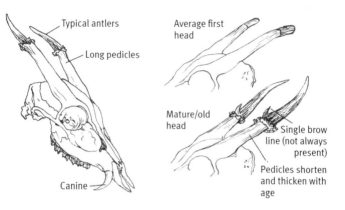

Typical antlers

Long pedicles

Canine

Average first head

Mature/old head

Single brow line (not always present)

Pedicles shorten and thicken with age

Heads of the Smaller Deer for Comparison

Left: Muntjac buck in velvet of second head

Centre: Water deer buck

Right: Roe buck in velvet

Inset: Roe buck with perruque head due to injury to testicles

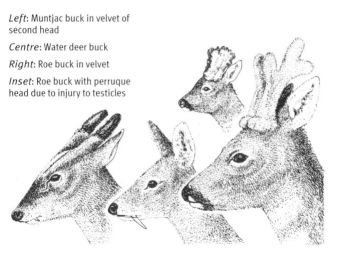

Ways of Determining Age

As antlers are not a safe criterion of age, other methods of age determination can be applied. The different deer species attain full adult dentition at given ages, after which their teeth are not replaced. Wear on teeth is one way of making an approximate judgement, but this can vary according to the habitat. The teeth of a deer that feeds heavily on rough material or in grittier environments will wear down faster than those of an animal that lives under less demanding conditions, but of course it is impossible to examine the teeth of a live wild deer.

As deer age they tend to follow similar kinds of development as a human being – youth and sprightliness giving way to middle age and "spread", then well-developed and rounded hind quarters. Eventually the curves disappear, joints stiffen, and senility starts to become apparent. However, just like humans, some deer defy the rules.

Beyond obviously immature animals in their first year, for which birthing dates are well known, it is generally unrealistic to precisely determine the exact age of a living, grown animal (unless it has been visibly tagged at birth) so it is far better to think in terms of young, mature and old.

The table below offers some general guidelines on determining the age of a deer though it is stressed that *not all signs are absolute*. Beware particularly that animals in their thicker winter coat may look misleadingly more heavily built. It should be noted that there may be some minor variations between species and, as the different species have different typical lifespans and effective breeding ages, age groups should be taken as:

	Large deer species	Roe & muntjac	Water deer
Young	Not yet 3 yrs	Not yet 3 yrs	Not yet 1 yr
Mature	Not yet 9 yrs	Not yet 7 yrs	Not yet 5 yrs
Old	Over 9 yrs	Over 7 yrs	Over 5 yrs

	Young	Mature	Old
Seasonal			
Coat change	Earliest	Later	Latest
Antler casting & growth	Latest	Earlier	Earliest
Appearance			
Antler form	Light and simple	Fully developed	Reduced, thicker beam, "going back"
Canine tusk (water deer bucks only)	Not visible	Visible	Visible
Body	Slim	Muscled	Heavy
Neck	Thin	Firm & muscled	Heavy
Back	Straight	Level, slight dip	Dipping
Belly	Taut	Dropping slightly	Sagging
Rump	Narrow	Rounded	Well-filled (but may become bony with advancing age)
Facial expression	Trusting	Alert & wary	Suspicious
General			
Gait	Light & brisk	Deliberate	Stiff
Behaviour	Playful, curious & unwary	Purposeful	Cautious
Reaction to potential threat	Incautious, may investigate	Alert, staring & quickly reactive	As mature (very old animals may become less alert)
Feeding	Incautious	Alert	Very wary

Ageing in Roe Buck

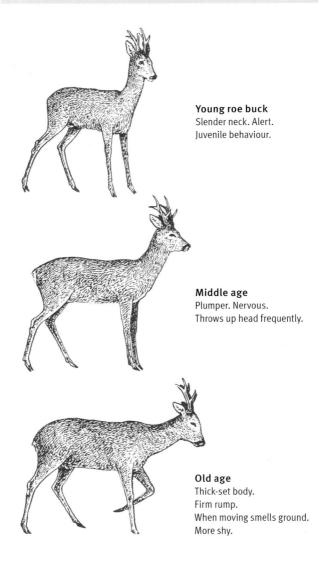

Young roe buck
Slender neck. Alert.
Juvenile behaviour.

Middle age
Plumper. Nervous.
Throws up head frequently.

Old age
Thick-set body.
Firm rump.
When moving smells ground.
More shy.

SEASONAL CHANGE OF COAT

Deer shed their heavier winter coat in spring, and as winter again approaches they develop a thicker one. This seasonal change often involves a change of colour. Although it is impossible to mention every variation that might be encountered, the most important ones for each species are given. Any notable differences seen are well worth recording.

Fawns, kids and calves are generally spotted, which provides a protective camouflage in the shade where sunlight filters through the surrounding vegetation.

RED DEER

Summer: considerable variation occurs. Grey, dark reddish brown, deep brown or buff coats may be seen. The inner sides of the thighs are creamy yellow and the rump light grey. A line of dark hair is sometimes found down the back. The tail is tufted and about 15 cm long. A well-developed mane is produced by stags before the rutting period in September. Older stags retain this mane throughout the year but younger ones lose much of it when the winter coat is shed in May.

Winter: coat rough and thick, dark brown, greyish brown or grey in colour, and often looks dirty especially after wallowing (see second page of colour section). Change of coat commences in May; at this time tufts of shed hair may be found in wallows.

Calf: dark brown on back and flanks and spotted with white. Spots lost within around six weeks as uniform dull brown fluffy coat is grown.

SIKA

Summer: flanks a warm, buff brown, spotted with yellowish white though rather less conspicuously than in the common variety of fallow. Usually a row of white spots on either side of dark dorsal stripe. Stags are darker than hinds. The dark stripe is usually continued as a line down the dorsal surface of white tail. Characteristic white hairs over the metatarsal gland on hind legs.

Winter: longer and darker coat, sooty brown above and greyish brown below, without spots. Stags look almost black from a distance. Hinds conspicuously grey. Head paler and grey at all times. Black-edged white rump patch is very conspicuous in both summer and winter and expands noticeably when the animal is startled or takes flight.

In comparison, fallow (common variety) tail is much longer and blacker on the dorsal side. Characteristic U-shaped eyebrow stripe, lighter in colour than rest of head.

Calf: born in summer coat but browner than adult, with fewer spots and much reduced caudal disc.

FALLOW DEER

There are four main colour varieties with many intermediate forms.

Common: various shades of chestnut with prominent cream or white spots in summer. In winter they become darker and the spots are lost. Rump white, edged with black inverted horseshoe shape. Black line runs down back and to tip of tail.

Menil: as above but spots retained in winter. Rather brighter colours than common. Edge of rump and dorsal surface of tail brown.

Black: dark chocolate to almost intense black. No white rump. Spots occasionally visible at close quarters. Slightly greyer in winter.

White: an overall cream colour. Frequently seen in parks where selective breeding is common. True albinos are rare.

In all colour varieties the change to a thicker winter coat occurs during October. Summer pelage is regained in the following May.

Fawns: common and menil have large white spots. Black fawns may have spots faintly visible. White fawns only show a difference in tone where spots should be.

ROE DEER

Summer: a bright reddish brown, flanks and belly paler. Dark muzzle with grey patches on either side and white spots below nostrils (not always present). Ears large and black bordered. Horizontally oval almost buff rump with no black markings. No visible tail.

Casting of coat begins in April and continues into May or even later.

Winter: coat starts to grow in October and continues into November. Pelage becomes greyish brown or even grey and is composed of long brittle wavy hairs. Face and sides of head darker. One or two lighter patches (gorget patches) may occur on front of neck. Caudal disc is now very visibly white and is erectile at times of stress. Does have an obvious white anal tuft (tush). Does are also distinguishable by shape of caudal disc which is heart shaped compared to kidney shape of buck. White, melanistic or skewbald varieties occur very rarely.

Kid: light brown much flecked with white. Becomes dull uniform brown within about six weeks and develops into adult winter coat during the autumn following birth.

MUNTJAC

Summer: a glossy bay with an orange tint to the face and chest, doe sometimes appears greyer and browner. The tail is ginger above and raised to display white underside when alarmed. Legs are dark in both summer and winter. Summer pelage is fully developed by May.

Winter: the only slightly heavier grey-brown winter coat is fully grown by November and has no undercoat. Tail remains same as in summer. Antler pedicles have a dark brown stripe on the medial side giving the appearance of a V shape; does have a dark brown crown patch.

Fawn: dark brown with light-coloured spots and a clear strip of chestnut-coloured hair down the back. Adult pelage is assumed at around eight weeks old.

WATER DEER

Summer: a uniform sandy colour or light reddish brown with lighter under parts. Head and ears buff with greyish band across the muzzle. White around nose, eyes, chin and inside ears. Small tail and no visible rump patch.

Winter: coat heavier and a darker sandy grey with a "salt and pepper" look. Individual hairs are coarse, hollow, about 40–55 mm in length and whitish over most of the length. It is loose and easily dislodged, and readily found (often in tufts) where water deer occur.

Fawn: colour varies between dark brown and reddish, with two rows of faint pale spots

See also the colour plate section between pp 80 and 81.

GAIT AND MOVEMENT

Each of the deer species has typical manners of movement along with recognisable aspects of their gait. These are often related to the age of the animal along with other aspects of its development (see *Tracks* pages 18-25). Some of these characteristics are shown below in diagram form.

RED DEER

Red deer usually move with a characteristic trot, with the head generally held erect and steady. The overall movement has a dignified and steady rhythm. In forest conditions the head of a stag is often thrown back with the antlers along each side of the body.

The even-striding trot can break into a canter or gallop or reduce to a steady walk. A 6 ft fence is readily cleared with a single jump by fully grown adults, but young deer may struggle with lesser heights. There is a special danger of a hind leg becoming trapped between top strands of stock fences.

SIKA

When first alarmed a sika tends to stand and face the cause of disturbance, occasionally stamping with a forefoot and craning its neck. It may then advance raising each leg hesitantly with the foot facing forward. If alarm decreases the animal will turn rapidly by jumping with all feet together as if on springs, before making off. After a short distance is covered it often stops, advances with a stilted gait, and retreats again. Advance and retreat may continue for some time unless the animal is seriously disturbed, at which point it will gallop away like other deer.

FALLOW DEER

Move with a less rapid trot than red deer. When first disturbed they often appear nervy and indecisive. Smaller parties depart for cover at a steady, easy gallop and in single file. When seriously alarmed fallow bounce away with all four legs held stiff and leaving the ground at the same time, a gait known as "pronking", before stopping briefly at a safe distance and then continuing at a rapid canter.

ROE DEER

When undisturbed, roe move with great delicacy and care, silently pushing their way through undergrowth and often with nose to the ground, at a slow walk. If necessary this movement breaks quickly into a trot or canter. Sudden disturbance may provoke a characteristic bounding gallop which brings the head above the surrounding herbage and allows a view of what is ahead. This is often accompanied by barking.

On reaching safety a roe will frequently stop and look back before disappearing into cover. When really alarmed, and when the need arises, a roe can creep away almost flat along the ground. This ability is also used to get under a wire fence or other narrow space. A 5 ft jump is readily achieved.

MUNTJAC

The normal gait can be a cautious, bird-like movement, a pottering walk with head held low, a swinging motion, or a sprint at great speed. Muntjac traverse dense undergrowth with ease and have been known to clear obstacles well in excess of 5 ft. When disturbed, they often run with the tail held erect to display the white underside.

WATER DEER

Relaxed water deer feeding in the open may stop to scan their surroundings regularly. A suspicious animal will raise its head into an upright position and stare attentively with ears pricked while remaining quite still, occasionally moving the head up and down or side to side, sometimes for just a few seconds but often for several minutes. If alarmed it will either run or bound away, in the latter gait flinging up the hind legs. Sometimes an alarmed animal may crouch or try to blend into the background, even when in the open.

FOOD AND FEEDING

Deer are herbivorous ruminants which chew the cud, and as such feed almost exclusively on plant matter. On odd occasions they have, however, been known to eat other items and have even been observed taking the eggs and chicks of ground nesting birds albeit very rarely. All deer will also chew cast antlers, presumably for their mineral content. Signs of feeding activity are often helpful in identifying the species present.

RED DEER

In woodlands, red deer will feed on most herbs, grasses and mosses. Grasses make up a major part of the diet throughout the year in most habitats. Acorns, beech mast, sweet chestnuts, hawthorn, rowan berries and other seasonal fruits are also taken in autumn. Bramble, ivy, holly and yew can become major parts of the winter diet. They are rough and noisy browsers, tearing down vegetation up to 6 ft (180 cm) above the ground and breaking branches with their antlers. They also damage pole-size trees by stripping bark to heights of between 4½ft and 5 ft (135–150 cm). They will also feed in open fields among crops such as spring wheat and root crops, particularly during cold weather. Such damage may occur throughout the year where their home ranges adjoin farmland. On open moorland and deer forest whortleberry, heather and rough grasses form the main diet. Near the sea, seaweed may be taken during visits to the shore.

SIKA

Feeding habits may vary according to different areas. A predominantly grazing habit will concentrate on grass and rough herbage; elsewhere the leaves of broad-leaved tree species or conifer needles may be taken. Sika appear especially fond of hazel shoots and the branches of medium-sized trees of other species are often stripped. Food crops may also be raided where they are available. In coastal areas the shoots of sea couch grass can be much sought after.

FALLOW DEER

Food is very similar to that of woodland red deer but fallow may roam over wider areas in search of it, with grasses making up an important part of their diet. They often feed on the move. They are especially fond of crab apples, chestnuts and berries of all kinds when they are available. Young shoots of holly and bramble, and tree branches (especially ash and thorn) attract them. They are also given to marauding in crops or raiding gardens. In woodlands the stripping of bark is, as a rule, confined to smooth barked hardwoods to a height of about 4 ft (120 cm). Scrapes are made in search of truffles.

ROE DEER

Selective browsers which take a wide variety of leaves and berries, and there are few plants among the habitat of roe that are not used for food at some time or another. They are very fond of blackberry, wild rose and juniper but do not confine themselves to one specific food plant for very long and will move steadily from one to another while feeding, appearing to seek out the more succulent parts with great care. Fungi, pine shoots, young heather and the emerging fronds of ferns are just a few of the items in a very varied diet. Bracken appears to be taken only rarely (if ever). Likewise, bark is also only rarely stripped, although this is more likely in severe weather. Roe can also do serious damage to vegetable patches and flower beds in gardens.

MUNTJAC

The staple diet is bramble, ivy, tree shoots and a wide range of woodland flowers. Wild fruits are taken in season. Muntjac only occasionally significant agricultural or forestry damage, but heavy populations can thin the understoreys of woodland and cause environmental issues. They will also take a wide variety of garden plants including roses and tulips, as well as vegetables such as brassicas and beans, if given the opportunity.

WATER DEER

Like the muntjac, the water deer has a relatively simple diges-
tive system that is less efficient than that of the larger deer at
processing plant fibre so they are more reliant on selecting
the more nutritious food items. They feed widely on grasses
and sedges but select the tips of blades rather than cropping
the plant closer to the ground. Other browse items may also
include bramble, ferns, buckthorn, ivy and sallow. Berries are
eaten when available. Damage has also been noted in fields
containing crops such as winter wheat, carrots or oilseed rape.

MAXIMUM BROWSING HEIGHTS		
Species	**Normal**	**Standing on hind legs**
Red	1.5 m	1.9 m
Sika	1.4 m	1.8 m
Fallow	1.4 m	1.7 m
Roe	1.15 m	1.5 m
Muntjac	1.0 m	1.25 m
Water deer	1.0 m	Not observed

HABITS AND HERD ACTIVITIES

Understanding the behaviour of the different deer species is greatly helpful in identifying them, but it also helps to know when to look out for characteristic activities. This section looks at some seasonal activities and should be read in conjunction with the charts on pages 69-73.

RED DEER

Although a gregarious species, herd composition changes according to the time of year. Mixed herds of stags, hinds, young deer and calves may be regularly encountered, particularly in the Highlands of Scotland, during summer and winter. Only in late spring and early summer do mature stags and hinds tend to separate fully.

The oldest stags tend to live apart from the main herds. During the rut they compete to obtain possession of hinds; before this period they can travel over very large distances. Wallows made in peat or muddy pools are used by both sexes at any time of year but most frequently during autumn when extensive scent marking occurs at the wallows and surrounding trees. Large amounts of cast hair can be found in wallowing areas around April.

Any approach to a new or suspicious object is made from downwind (this is a useful consideration when siting a hide for photography or deer watching). If alarmed, the hind runs with the calf and if danger persists she may push it into thick undergrowth where it lies absolutely still.

Feeding is most intensive during early morning and at night, with shorter feeding bouts in between resting and rumination during the day. The day is mainly spent lying up in cover or other areas where the deer feels relatively safe. In the evening it can be productive to watch for movement from cover towards feeding grounds, or near water in glens and river valleys.

SIKA

Not exceptionally gregarious, even when numerous, and under most circumstances groups of more than 20 are uncommon except in late winter and early spring. Smaller groups are more usual. Mixed herds of stags and hind are fairly common in winter, otherwise separate in small parties. Stags can be very secretive and seldom seen, often moving largely in darkness.

During the rut stags fight for possession of hinds, adopting rutting stands in the manner of fallow deer or alternately attempting to round up parcels of hinds like red deer. Wallows are made.

Daily activity is superficially similar to that of red deer, with which they are occasionally seen where ranges overlap. Fraying activity is similar to fallow deer and there may be much thrashing of heather or gorse which leaves characteristic devastation on the boundaries of territories. Within territories a master stag may thrash out a rutting stand which might be in roughly the same place each year. Bole scoring may become habitual and can lead to serious damage.

When moving out to feed, small groups may converge into larger parties of twelve or more. Within an hour or two of dawn they return to the thickest available cover or lie up in standing crops. Sika are most likely to be seen in early morning or late evening, feeding in open woodland, heathland, moorland or farmland. In midwinter they can become almost entirely nocturnal but may move out to graze during the day throughout the year where unmolested.

In autumn, winter and spring, small family parties of a hind, her current calf and the previous year's, are usual associations.

These can join to form groups of up to around a dozen animals. At eight to nine months old, stag calves join the stag parties, while hind calves remain with their mothers for around a year. After the rut, stags feed for a short time with hinds but gradually form separate parties towards the end of the year.

FALLOW DEER

Gregarious: may form aggregations of 150 and more in some open areas, but disperse into smaller more persistent social groups of one to three adult females and their current and sometimes previous year's offspring when in cover.

Mud wallowing as seen by red deer is relatively rare, but bucks will create mud scrapes which they scent mark and urinate into. During the rut the bucks challenge each other and may fight. Assembly points may be found where worn areas with many tracks encircle a fraying stock or rubbing tree, or stamping may occur on the ground against some prominent object, with the animals depositing scent mainly from their preorbital and interdigital glands near the eyes and feet. Scrapes like those of roe deer are made but they are larger, deeper, and often also show marks made by the antler brow tine.

Daily activity resembles that of red deer. Much of the day is spent in relative inactivity lying up in bracken, thorn scrub or other cover but where undisturbed they will often lie out in sunlight. If danger threatens they make off in single file. At dusk they move out to feed in woodland rides and fields.

Thrashing of young trees and bushes occurs during the rut. The scoring of bark and fraying are additional means by which the buck marks out his temporary territory and sets his scent.

ROE DEER

Non-gregarious as a rule and generally only seen singly, in small family parties or as rutting pairs. Larger parties may build up during the winter. Normally a woodland deer, the roe is adaptable and may live in such diverse places as open moors, farmland with hedgerow cover, or within the peri-urban fringe.

Roe can be inquisitive animals and may not always move away when first disturbed. They may even remain lying at a safe distance from forestry or agricultural activities, or road traffic, apparently undisturbed.

During the rut the doe leads the buck in a pursuit which starts slowly but becomes increasingly avid. The chase often focuses into running in a circle around a focal point. Prior to this the buck marks his territory, from April onwards, fraying trees on its border and leaving scent from the glands between the antlers and below the eyes on stems and leaves.

Play areas, often with obvious circles and figure of eight tracks, are used by does and kids in June and early July. Fraying of young trees to a height of around 60 cm often occurs when velvet is being removed in early spring – as a general rule, the thicker the tree and longer the fraying marks, the older and possibly the more dominant the buck. Pawing the ground with the cleaves of the feet leaves characteristic scrapes which help to identify the presence of this deer. Thrashing of tall plants such as willow herb also occurs.

In defence of its territory the buck pursues all other roe-buck intruders aggressively; short and sometimes lethal battles can take place. Mating takes place between late July and early August, the doe being in heat only during this short period. Roe are unusual among deer in that the fertilised egg only starts to develop normally from December onwards; this is known as delayed implantation. Twin kids are not uncommon, frequently one of each sex, and triplets may be produced in good years.

MUNTJAC

Most frequently encountered alone, or as doe and accompanying fawn, or rutting pairs. Two adult females seen together are likely to be mother and daughter with overlapping ranges. Small informal groups may sometimes be seen in favoured feeding areas where local densities are high. Mutual grooming occurs between adult pairs. A disturbed muntjac will bound away with its tail held vertically to display the white underside.

The muntjac is the only UK deer species to breed continuously throughout the year with fawns produced at seven-month intervals. Mating occurs shortly after the birth of the single fawn. Muntjac tend to live and feed in deep cover and their behaviour can be difficult to observe.

Bucks fray the bark of small shoots and saplings, primarily with the lower incisors, normally at a height of between 20 cm and 40 cm but sometimes up to 60 cm.

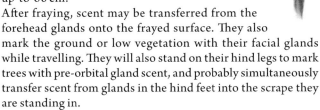

After fraying, scent may be transferred from the forehead glands onto the frayed surface. They also mark the ground or low vegetation with their facial glands while travelling. They will also stand on their hind legs to mark trees with pre-orbital gland scent, and probably simultaneously transfer scent from glands in the hind feet into the scrape they are standing in.

They also scrape the ground vigorously with their forefeet as another form of territorial marking; scrapes can measure as much as a metre across, often with hoof prints and droppings on the surface.

Of all the UK deer, muntjac seem to habituate the most readily to human presence and are increasingly reported living within the urban fringe and in well-vegetated or overgrown habitats within towns and cities.

WATER DEER

Like muntjac and roe, water deer are a more solitary species. Larger groups can be encountered outside wetlands in the early months of the year, when individuals congregate at favourable feeding areas. Loose aggregations can also be encountered on agricultural land supporting larger populations. Otherwise, apart from during the December rut or when in family groups (litters of up to seven fawns are possible from one birthing, but two to three are more usual), they are more usually seen alone.

Habitat resembling that in their native Asia, such as the scrubby reed beds of East Anglia, seems optimal, but water deer are adaptable and can be found on grazing marshes and arable land as well as in woodland. They are less tolerant of human presence than muntjac and seldom encountered in semi-urban areas.

As the rut approaches bucks will become more strongly territorial and scent mark vegetation using facial glands. They may also fray thin plant or tree stems using the inside of their canine tusks. Females only show interest in being territorial prior to giving birth. A buck without a territory may try to displace a rival.

As water deer do not possess antlers, fighting between bucks involves "dancing" around each other while each attempts to land a blow with either a forefoot or tusk. Such fights tend to be brief and may be preceded by parallel walking, which often ends with one animal giving way and departing. Some fights can, however, be intense and may end in the death of one protagonist.

SEASONAL BEHAVIOUR

The diagrams that follow represent as closely as possible the main features of yearly activity, although there will inevitably be some variations. The period of maximum activity is represented by a solid bar, while lighter shading indicates earlier and later periods of activity.

These diagrams are based on the most recent information available at the time of publication so may be slightly at variance with other reference sources.

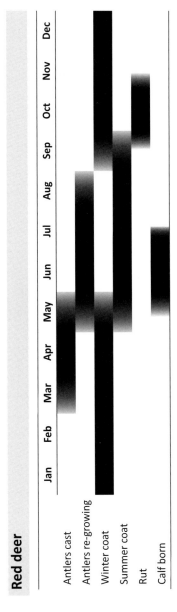

Red deer

Sika

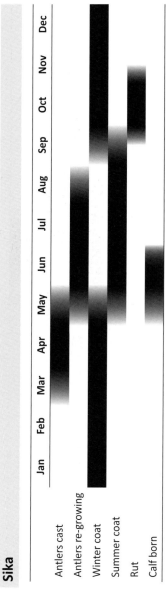

	Jan	Feb	Mar	Apr	May	Jun	Jul	Aug	Sep	Oct	Nov	Dec
Antlers cast												
Antlers re-growing												
Winter coat												
Summer coat												
Rut												
Calf born												

Fallow deer

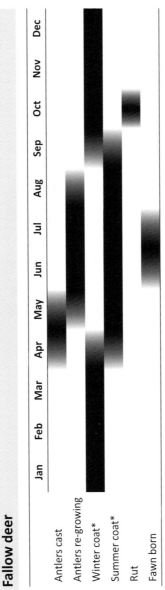

	Jan	Feb	Mar	Apr	May	Jun	Jul	Aug	Sep	Oct	Nov	Dec
Antlers cast												
Antlers re-growing												
Winter coat*												
Summer coat*												
Rut												
Fawn born												

*Menil and other dark-coated forms of fallow deer may keep the same coat year round.

Roe deer

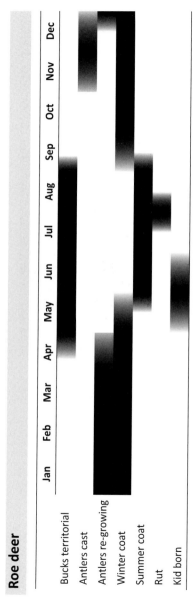

	Jan	Feb	Mar	Apr	May	Jun	Jul	Aug	Sep	Oct	Nov	Dec
Bucks territorial												
Antlers cast												
Antlers re-growing												
Winter coat												
Summer coat												
Rut												
Kid born												

Muntjac

	Jan	Feb	Mar	Apr	May	Jun	Jul	Aug	Sep	Oct	Nov	Dec
Antlers cast												
Antlers re-growing												
Winter coat												
Summer coat												
Rut												
Fawn born												

Notes: 1. May rut and give birth at any time of year.

2. Immature bucks in velvet or hard antler might be encountered at any time of year.

Water deer

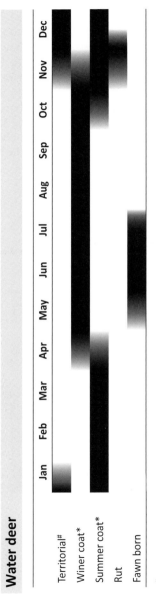

	Jan	Feb	Mar	Apr	May	Jun	Jul	Aug	Sep	Oct	Nov	Dec
Territorial#												
Winer coat*												
Summer coat*												
Rut												
Fawn born												

#Territoriality is poorly documented in the UK, and may be adopted variably by both sexes at different times of year
*Moulting dates are highly variable

74

DEER DISTRIBUTION

The following maps show the distribution of the UK's deer species recorded in 10 x 10 km squares. A few records, and especially the more isolated ones, may now be historic as deer presence can be transitory. Updated maps are regularly produced and can be found on the BDS website at bds.org.uk.

There may be unrecorded deer presence elsewhere. Reports of new sightings are always welcomed by the BDS, either by email or through the free Deer App which can be downloaded from the Information and Advice section of the BDS website.

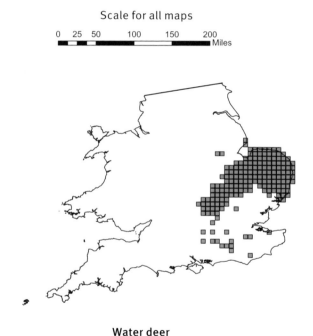

Scale for all maps

Water deer

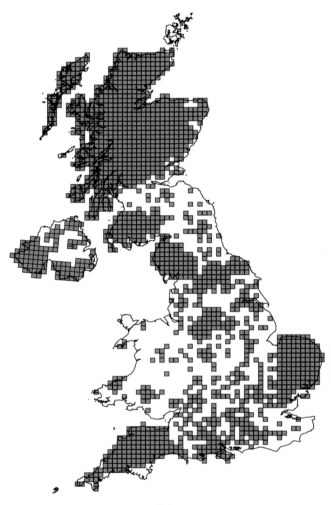

Red deer

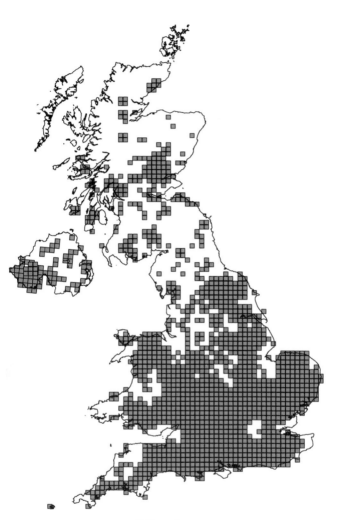

Fallow deer

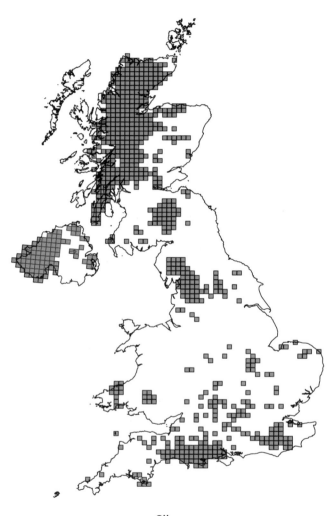

Sika

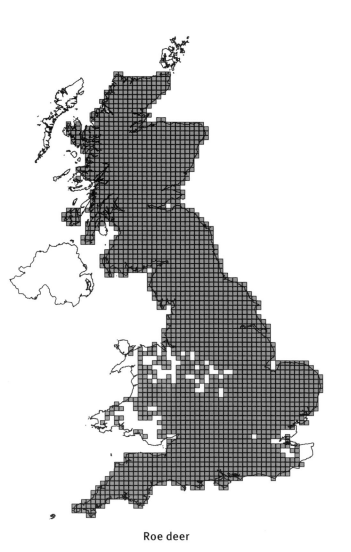

Roe deer

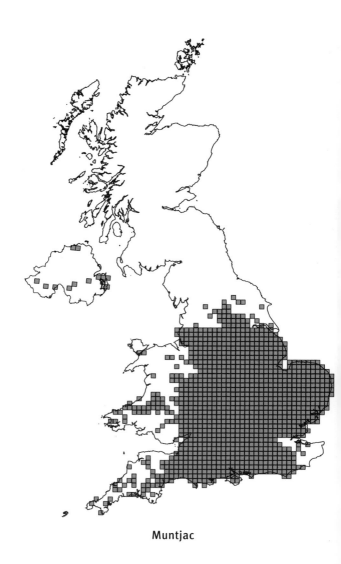

Muntjac

Red deer – Stag in summer coat

Red deer – Hind in winter coat

Fallow deer – Common and white bucks in summer coat

Fallow deer – A young menil buck in summer coat

Fallow deer – Common variety doe in winter coat

Fallow deer – Black variety bucks in winter coat

Sika – Mature and two younger stags in summer coat

Sika – Stag in winter coat

Roe deer – A mixed group of roe in winter coat

Roe deer – Doe in summer coat

Muntjac – Doe in summer coat showing length of tail

Muntjac – Buck in summer coat, starting to regrow his antlers

Water deer – Doe in winter coat

Water deer – Buck in summer coat

GLOSSARY

Many of the words used to describe deer and their habits are derived from ancient hunting language, the "Terms of Venery", and may be unfamiliar. In most cases they were originally specific to the red and fallow deer, which were the most important species to the medieval hunter, but since those times they have come to be applied to other species as well. In case of confusion, some of those still in more common usage are listed below. There are many more that have fallen out of use, and some may only be encountered in certain parts of the country.

It is normal practice to use the "deer" suffix when referring to red, fallow, roe and water deer, though unnecessary for sika or muntjac as both of the latter words are taken from those meaning "deer" in the language of their countries of origin (Japanese and Sunda).

The genders and offspring of the UK's deer have different names depending on the species – they are:

Species	Male	Female	Young
Red deer	Stag	Hind	Calf
Sika	Stag	Hind	Calf
Fallow deer	Buck	Doe	Fawn
Roe deer	Buck	Doe	Kid
Muntjac	Buck	Doe	Fawn
Water deer	Buck	Doe	Fawn

IDENTIFICATION

Albino – A deer with an absence of the pigment melanin in its hair and skin, which are white, and its eyes, which are red or blue. Complete albinism is rare.

Antler – A temporary growth of bony material carried on top of the skull, usually shed and regrown annually. Antlers are normally grown only by male deer although female reindeer also habitually produce them. During the growth period they are covered in *velvet* which dies back when the antler is fully grown and shed by fraying on bushes or trees. Antlers should not be confused with *horns*.

The Attire of a Red Stag (after Herbert Fooks)

A Royal has three on top and "all his rights", ie, brow, bay and tray tines

Length is measured from highest point to lower edge of coronet girth at narrowest point between bay and tray

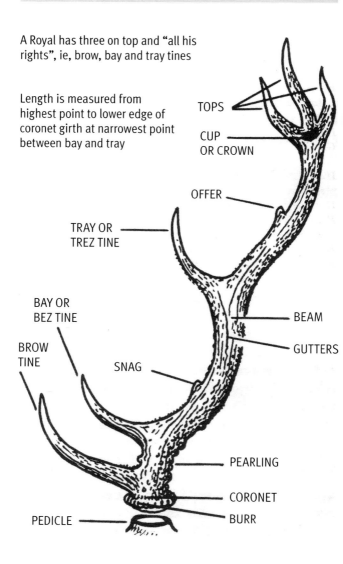

TOPS

CUP OR CROWN

OFFER

TRAY OR TREZ TINE

BAY OR BEZ TINE

BROW TINE

SNAG

BEAM

GUTTERS

PEARLING

CORONET

PEDICLE

BURR

Buck – A male fallow, roe or muntjac. Among fallow, a bare buck is a four year old and a great buck is an animal of five years or over. See also **pricket**, **sore** and **sorel**.

Calf – The young of sika and red deer in their first year.

Caudal patch – The white or paler coloured rear end of a deer located beneath its tail. Also known as the **speculum** or **target**.

Crotties – Heaps of droppings of deer (see also **fewmets**).

Doe – A female fallow, roe or muntjac.

Fawn – Strictly speaking a young fallow or muntjac in its first year, but often generally used to describe the young of all deer species in their first year.

Fewmets – Individual droppings of deer.

Gorget – The white throat patch of a roe deer, most apparent in winter **pelage**.

Hart – An alternative to the term **stag**, now outmoded and seldom used.

Havier – A castrated stag.

Head – A general term used to describe the antlers of deer, usually when referring to their size, conformation and appearance.

Hind – A female sika or red deer.

Horn – As opposed to **antlers**, horns are bony outgrowths from the skull of cattle, goats, sheep etc that continue to grow throughout an animal's life and are sheathed in keratin, the same material found in finger and toenails. In parts of Scotland **antlers** are sometimes referred to as horns.

Hummel – A male deer, usually red, that has failed to produce antlers. Also known as a **nott** in the southwest of England.

Imperial – A largely outmoded term for a red deer stag with fourteen points (seven on each side) with the top three forming a cup or crown.

Kid – The young of a roe deer in its first year.

Knobber – Male red deer in its second year.

Leucism/leucistic – Paler than usual colouration caused by under-production of melanin (see **albino**).

Melanistic – A deer with a darker than normal pelage; usually linked to over-production of the pigment melanin.

Menil – Colour variety of fallow deer which remains spotted in its winter pelage.

Nott – See **hummel**.

Palm – The flattened portion of the **antler** of a fallow deer.

Pelage – The coat of a deer or other animal.

Perruque – Malformation of antlers caused by accidental castration, or another interruption to the supply of the male hormone testosterone, soon after antler casting. This results in uncontrolled antler growth which produces heavy masses of spongy tissue covered in velvet instead of normal antlers.

Pricket – Male sika or fallow deer in its second year.

Royal – A red deer stag with twelve points (six on each side) with the top three forming a cup or crown (hence "royal").

Sore – A three-year-old fallow buck.

Sorel – A two-year-old fallow buck.

Speculum – See **caudal patch**.

Spellers – The top and rear points along the palm of a fallow deer's antlers.

Stag – A male sika or red deer.

Switch – An adult red deer stag with no points above the brow **tine**. A "clean switch" does not even possess brow tines.

Target – See **caudal patch**.

Tine – A branch of growth from an **antler**.

Tush – A downward-pointing tuft of hair at the base of the rump patch of a roe doe. Also an archaic term for the canine tooth of a red deer.

Velvet – A thin, sensitive skin that covers growing **antlers**, protecting them and supplying them with blood.

Voice – A red deer "roars" or "bells".

　　　　A sika stag "whistles".

　　　　A fallow buck "groans" or "belches".

　　　　A roe buck "barks" or "bells".

　　　　A muntjac or water deer of either sex "barks".

Waster – An ailing deer in poor condition, usually as a result of injury, malnutrition or disease.

Yeld – A mature female deer that has not produced offspring but is not necessarily barren.

HABITS

Browsing – Feeding on the leaves, shoots or twigs of a tree or shrub, usually selectively, as opposed to **grazing** on plant material at ground level.

Burnishing – A term more specific to the New Forest that describes the process of cleaning **antlers** of **velvet**. Very often continued after velvet has been removed.

Cast/casting – When a deer sheds its ***antlers***.

Cleaning – A general term for the ***fraying*** off of ***velvet*** from the ***antlers*** on trees, bushes, heather etc. See also ***fraying stock***.

Couch – A deer's bedding place.

Entry – Gap made by a deer in a thicket, hedge or fence.

Fraying – Damage caused to vegetation by a deer when cleaning its ***antlers*** or marking territory.

Fraying stock – A bush, tree or other object used by a deer for ***fraying***.

Gallery – Path worn by deer in close cover, especially applied to a series of parallel routes. See also ***rack***.

Grazing – Feeding on grasses, sedges, herbs or lichens that grow at ground level, as opposed to ***browsing*** on plant material found above the ground.

Harbour – The place where a deer, more specifically a red stag, lies in thick cover.

Home range – The area that an animal habitually travels within during its daily activities; not to be confused with ***territory***.

Lair or ligging – Largely obsolete terms for the actual place where a deer lies down. A red deer "harbours" or if disturbed is "unharboured", a fallow "lodges" and is "roused", and a roe "beds" and is "dislodged".

Parcel – A group of red hinds. The term is sometimes also applied to sika hinds.

Pollarding – A New Forest term for the casting of antlers.

Rack – The path worn by deer through regular use.

Ring – A circular path worn by deer around a focal point (see p 14).

Rubbing – Damage caused to a tree by a deer casting its coat.

Rut – The period prior to and including the mating activities of deer, during which characteristic behaviour occurs annually. Also used to describe the act of mating.

Rutting stand – The area within the territory of a stag or buck where rutting behaviour occurs annually.

Sanctuary – The part of a deer's territory or home range containing the ***lair***.

Scrape – A patch of ground scraped by deer with their feet as part of territorial demarcation activity; usually associated with ***fraying stocks***.

Stripping – The damage caused to trees by deer gnawing on their bark.

Territory – A defined area of habitat that an animal will attempt to claim the exclusive use of, usually for breeding purposes.

Thrash/thrashing – The act of a male deer beating trees or bushes with his **antlers**.

Wallow – Where a deer rolls in a muddy pool or peat hag (see p 14).

TRACKS

Cleaves – Two halves of the hoof or slot representing the principal toes.

Creep – Worn place under wire or other fence where deer have passed through.

Dew claws – Vestiges of two toes set above and behind the cleaves. Also known archaically as sur-cleaves, or ergots in the case of a stag.

Foil – The tracks of a deer on grass. See also **slot**.

Gait – The style and manner of movement.

Heel trail – A trail followed in the opposite direction to that in which it was made.

Misprint – To step irregularly, or failure to register.

Pace – The speed of movement as measured by the length of **step** or **stride**.

Pattern – The arrangement of footprints in the trail; variation dependant on **gait**.

Register – To place the hind foot in the slot made by the fore.

Signs – The means by which to judge the species, size, age and sex of a deer. They include the **step**, the **entry**, the **fewmets** and the **fraying stock**.

Slot – The foot and hoofprints of a deer in soft ground. Sometimes known as "view" in fallow and "foil" in roe.

Splay – The spread of the **cleaves**, particularly associated with soft ground.

Step – The interval between one hoofprint and the next.

Stride – The interval between successive impressions of the same foot.

Sway – The deviation of prints from the median line. These are most noticeable in a female deer at a later stage of pregnancy (see p 21).

Trail – The sequence of footprints and other signs marking the passage of a deer. Sometimes called the trace.

FORESTRY

Beat – An area of woodland or forestry under the jurisdiction of a forester.

Beating up – Replacing failed or lost tree crops in a plantation.

Brashing – Removal of lower branches in a plantation at the end of the thicket stage.

Canopy – Continuous cover formed by the crowns of woodland or forest trees.

Compartment – Sub-division of a forest defined for management purposes.

Coppice – Woodland cut back to encourage new growth for use as firewood, timber or other purposes.

Covert – Small woodland or thicket serving as a refuge for deer.

Establishment – The stage at which a forest crop is accepted as fully grown.

Final crop – The best trees of a plantation, selected to grow on to maturity.

High forest – A plantation continued in growth to mature stage after thinning.

Natural regeneration – The self-seeding of woodland or forest trees, in contrast to sowing or planting.

Pole crop – A plantation in the early stages of thinning.

Rack – A path cut through a young plantation to facilitate access.

Ride – A wide track or break separating a forest into blocks.

Thicket – The stage of growth between the closing of the canopy and first thinning.

Underplanting – The introduction of a new crop under the partial canopy of an older one.

DEER MANAGEMENT

Catch-up – The capture of deer for relocation, or at other times when they need to be handled. A license for this procedure is required by law.

Close Season – Times during the year when the taking or killing of deer is prohibited by law. These will vary according to species and sex. See p 88.

Conservation – The action necessary to protect deer and their habitat from exploitation or other pressures.

Cull – The act of removing surplus deer from a population, usually to balance age and sex groups while maintaining it in balance with the available habitat, or to meet other set management objectives.

Deer forest – As distinct from a forest of trees, the ancient Highland forests of Scotland, despite being long cleared of trees but still home to herds of deer, retain their former title of "forest". A few places in England and Ireland also retain the same designation.

Going back – Once a male deer is past its prime, its antlers may progressively diminish in size and are said to be "going back". Disease may produce a similar effect.

Gralloch – The removal of the internal organs of a deer after shooting as part of the process of producing **venison**.

High seat – An elevated structure used for observing or shooting deer. See p 34.

Management – The careful planning of conservation and/or control of a deer population. See also **cull**.

Moving – A procedure involving the moving of deer gently and without panic in a desired direction.

Paint – A New Forest term for a blood trail left by a deer that has been shot.

Selective shooting – The shooting of any deer which is old, diseased or injured, or whose removal would be to the benefit of the overall population in an area. See also **cull**.

Stalk – The quiet, unobserved approach to a deer for the purpose of observing, photographing or shooting.

Venison – The prepared meat of a deer.

Winter feeding – At times of bad prevailing conditions, or otherwise, when overcrowding might cause deaths from malnutrition, the provision of supplementary food during winter might become an essential part of management.

STATUTORY CLOSE SEASONS FOR DEER

The law specifies closed seasons when deer are protected and may not normally be taken, even by legal means. They tend to revolve around the critical breeding times for female deer and antler growth for males and vary between species due to seasonal differences in cycles. Muntjac can breed all year round and as such enjoy no close season. There may be circumstances, such as a need to deal with sick or injured deer, when culling is permitted during the Close Season.

At the time of writing the Close Seasons are as follows (all dates are inclusive) but may be subject to legislative change:

	England & Wales	Scotland	Northern Ireland
Red & sika males*	1 May – 31 July	21 October – 30 June	1 May – 31 July
Red & sika females*	1 April – 31 October	16 February – 20 October	1 April – 31 October
Fallow males	1 May – 31 July	1 May – 31 July	1 May – 31 July
Fallow females	1 April – 31 October	16 February – 20 October	1 April – 31 October
Roe males	1 November – 31 March	21 October – 31 March	Not present
Roe females	1 April– 31 October	1 April – 20 October	Not present
Water deer (both sexes)	1 April – 31 October	Not present	Not present
Muntjac (both sexes)	No Close Season		

* includes hybrids

INVASIVE ALIEN SPECIES
(ENFORCEMENT AND PERMITTING) ORDER 2019

Under this Order it is now illegal for anyone in possession of muntjac to let them breed, escape, be released or transported within the UK, or exported.

THE BRITISH DEER SOCIETY

Deer are keystone species that play a crucial role in the way that the UK's landscape functions. The British Deer Society [BDS] is a charity dedicated to educating and inspiring everyone about deer in their environment.

The BDS operates throughout the UK and through our education and research we raise awareness about wild deer and the issues surrounding them. We also provide training to actively ensure deer can be managed humanely and safely to the very highest of standards.

We want to ensure that wild deer in the UK are respected and valued, while being maintained in healthy and sustainable numbers, to benefit biodiversity and the wider environment.

You can support the BDS by:

Giving us a donation
Joining and becoming a member
Leaving us a gift in your will

To find out more, visit website at ***www.bds.org.uk*** or contact:

**The British Deer Society,
The Walled Garden, Burgate Manor,
Fordingbridge, Hampshire SP6 1EF**

**Telephone: 01425 655434
Email: info@bds.org.uk**

The BDS is a charity registered in England & Wales (No. 1069663) and in Scotland (No. SCO37817).

FURTHER RESOURCES

There is a wealth of literature relating to deer; the following books are recommended as a good starting point for anyone who wants to learn more about them. Some may be out of print but are still easily sourced.

General

CARNE, Peter. *Deer of Britain and Ireland: Their Origins and Distribution*. Swan Hill Press, Shrewsbury, 2000.

FLETCHER, John. *Deer*. Reaktion Books, London, 2014.

SMITH-JONES, Charles. *A Guide to the Deer of the World*. Quiller Publishing, Shrewsbury, 2022.

WHITEHEAD, G Kenneth. *The Whitehead Encyclopedia of Deer*. Swan Hill Press, Shrewsbury, 1993.

Biology and Ecology

GEIST, Valerius. *Deer of the World: Their Evolution, Behaviour and Ecology*. Swan Hill Press, Shrewsbury, 1999.

PUTMAN, Rory. *The Natural History of Deer*. Christopher Helm, Bromley, 1988.

Individual Species

CHAPMAN, Donald and CHAPMAN, Norma. *Fallow Deer: Their History, Distribution and Biology*. Terence Dalton, Lavenham, 1975.

COOKE, Arnold. *Muntjac and Water Deer*. Pelagic Publishing, Exeter, 2019.

PRIOR, Richard. *The Roe Deer: Conservation of a Native Species*. Swan Hill Press, Shrewsbury, 1995.

SMITH-JONES, Charles. *Muntjac: Managing an Alien Species*. Coch-y-Bonddu Books, Machynlleth, 2004.

Issues and Management

COLES, Charles L. *Gardens and Deer: A Guide to Damage Limitation*. Swan Hill Press, Shrewsbury, 1997.

GRIFFITHS, Dominic. *Deer Management in the UK*. Quiller Publishing, Shrewsbury, 2011.

PRIOR, Richard. *Trees and Deer*. Swan Hill Press, Shrewsbury, 1994.

SMITH-JONES, Charles. *Practical Deer Management.* Quiller Publishing, Shrewsbury, 2019.

Deer Watching & Photography

PRIOR, Richard. *Deer Watch.* Swan Hill Press, Shrewsbury, 1987.

ROUSE, Andy. (1999) *Photographing Animals in the Wild.* Fountain Press, Kingston-upon-Thames, 1999.

Legal

PARKES, Charlie and THORNLEY, John. *Deer: Law and Liabilities.* Quiller Publishing. Shrewsbury, 2008.

Websites

The British Deer Society: An informative website that includes information about British deer species and a searchable database of zoos, parks and other collections in the United Kingdom containing deer and open to the public. ***www.bds.org.uk***

iNaturalist: A social network for naturalists which allows sightings, photographs etc to be freely shared and discussed. ***www.inaturalist.org***

IUCN Red List: Comprehensive and authoritative listings of all world species of fauna and flora, with an extensive web page for each. ***www.iucnredlist.org***

Ultimate Ungulate: Reliable information and pictures of the world's ungulate species. ***www.ultimateungulate.com***

Coch-y-Bonddu Books: A good source for books on deer and their ecology, both new and out-of-print. All of the books in the reading lists may be obtained here. ***www.anglebooks.com***

Note: some websites may have greater longevity than others, but those above are active at the time of writing. Care should always be taken to consult reputable sources as some can be unreliable.

ACKNOWLEDGEMENTS

When the *Field Guide* was first produced it was inspired by a number of original members of the Mammal Society's Deer Group, many of whom went on to significantly advance our understanding of British deer through their research, writing and subsequent input to the BDS. The compiler and editor was F J "Jim" Taylor Page, and the original contributors were P H Carne, J S R Chard, Peter Delap, Herbert Fooks, Gerald Johnstone, Victor Ross, Henry Tegner and G Kenneth Whitehead.

In 1968 the copyright of the *Field Guide* was generously presented to the BDS by the Mammal Society, and the 1971 revised edition was produced with further specialist advice on the text from A Cadman, J McCurdy (N Ireland), M Clarke, F Courtier, O Dansie, M Horwood, J Hotchkis, J King, G Logan (Scotland), E Masters, F Mulloy (Eire), and D Talbot. It featured entirely new illustrations by Michael Clark, some of which can still be appreciated in this fourth edition.

This 2023 edition has been edited and revised by Charles Smith-Jones, on behalf of the BDS, with new illustrations especially produced for it by Katie Hargreaves. It is a testament to those who went before that there has been little need to amend much of the previous work but, to ensure that it is fully up to date, expert advice has been gratefully received from species specialists including Arnold Cooke, Jochen Langbein and Norma Chapman, and the seasonal activity charts were prepared by Alastair Ward and Nick Rout. Special thanks are also owed to Tom Logan for preparing the distribution maps. The BDS is also especially grateful to Paul Morgan, Caroline Oakley and designer Pete MacKenzie at Coch-y-Bonddu Books for their guidance and assistance in its preparation and printing.

The 1957 *Field Guide* met with immediate success, rapidly becoming an accepted handbook for both newcomers and experienced observers of deer. Achieving recognition as a compact, valuable and informative synthesis of concise facts and helpful detail, it was acknowledged as a textbook for foresters and those responsible for control, and a reference book for researchers and amateur naturalists alike, both in this country and abroad. We are confident that this remains true for the revised 2023 edition which coincides with the 60th anniversary of the BDS.